FIRST LIGHT

To David Miller
with my love
— Ethelbert Miller

FIRST LIGHT
NEW AND SELECTED POEMS

E. Ethelbert Miller

DuForcelf

First Light

Library of Congress Catalog Card No.: 93-074110

A DuForcelf book published by Black Classic Press, 1994

ISBN 0-933121-81-4

Cover Art by Frank Smith

Backcover photo © Julia Jones

Printed on acid free paper to assure long life

Founded in 1978, Black Classic Press specializes in bringing to light obscure and significant works by and about people of African descent. If our books are not available in your area, ask your local bookseller to order them. Our current list of titles can be obtained by writing:

Black Classic Press
c/o List
P.O. Box 13414
Baltimore, MD 21203

A Young Press With Some Very Old Ideas

For The Living: Denise, Jasmine-Simone, Nyere-Gibran
For Those Who Will Return: Egberto and Richard

These Poems Are First Light

Acknowledgements

Some poems in this anthology have previously appeared in the following books authored by Mr. Miller: *Andromeda, Migrant Worker, Season of Hunger/Cry of Rain, Where Are The Love Poems For Dictators?* Several have appeared in *The New Cavalcade* (edited by Arthur P. Davis, J. Saunders Redding and Joyce Ann Joyce) and *Black Erotica* (edited by Miriam DeCosta-Willis, Reginald Martin and Roseann P. Bell).

Selected poems have also been previously published in the following journals: *Black American Literature Forum, Washington Review, Gargoyle, Callaloo, The Stylus Anthology, 1989, Footwork '88, New Voices, New Concerns Newsletter, Konch, MAWA Tenth Annual Conference Souvenir Program, Black Scholar, The C.L.R. James Journal, Fear of Others/ La peur De L'Autre, Red Letters, Erewon, Black Buzzard Review, Sibanye!, Black Networking News, Catalyst.*

Cover art : *Celebration for Brother Paul Coates*

by Frank Smith

Frank Smith is an improvisational artist who brings the sensibility of jazz to his works. A native of Chicago, he has received numerous awards and honors within the United States and abroad. Since 1970, he has been a member of AFRICOBRA, a group of artists-activists that is dedicated to promoting and defining Afro-aesthetic principles in visual arts. He presently lives in Baltimore and teaches at the Maryland Institute of Art and Howard University.

Special Thanks To:

W. Paul Coates, Elanna Haywood, Heidi Marohn and Frank Smith

CONTENTS

BILL MAZEROSKI RETURNS
HOME FROM THE WORLD SERIES

GROW YOUR OWN CHINESE VEGETABLES

EL SALVADOR

INTRODUCTION

We Are Magic in Our Language: The Poetry of E. Ethelbert Miller

Poetry has a way of attaching itself to strangers. Most people do not read poetry but hear it on urban street corners from midnight to dawn. Our children, before their destruction by public education, share their dreams in the language of beginning poets. Young lovers, in their innocence, fight to find the language to express their love to each other: poetry. The best of our vocal groups sing and swing in poetry. Our classical "linguists" are our poets: Gwendolyn Brooks, Robert Hayden, Amiri Baraka, Mari Evans, Sonia Sanchez, Sterling Brown, Lucille Clifton, Melvin B. Tolson, Sterling Plumpp and Angela Jackson to name a few.

Black folks are not new to the language; we create and discard it daily whether it comes from gang members coding the language for secrecy or Baptist ministers opening the door to everlasting life in their Sunday morning sermons. However, it is our poets who study language. They preserve it, change it, melody it up, beautify it and give it back to the public as pictures of a complicated people and a difficult world. E. Ethelbert Miller paints the lives of his people in their unique and expressive tongue. For close to twenty years, Miller in his formidable but quiet manner has told and written poetry accenting the voices of his community with multicultural insights. In the pre-middle of his time, he gives us wild-memory, attached-sage, and sleeping lions speaking loudly in *First Light: New and Selected Poems.*

Much of *First Light* is autobiographical, a young boy growing into urban manhood; it's a book of family, of strangers, of learning to tell time by the people that populated his life. Mostly, it is a book of love, personal and cultural. Miller is not afraid to touch the one emotion that keeps all of us alive and productive. He travels in and out of love, but we do not feel any loss here. We feel that his loveships grow into friendships and whatever the outcome, family *remains.* He has scars; however new love does heal. Like the men who are not cowards to their feelings, he writes about many loves and makes them seeable. In seeing love, we too can approach love in a more holistic way.

The beauty of most selected poetry collections is that we read the poets' history. E. Ethelbert Miller's travels are complicated; like anthropologists, he joins the landscape of the cultures he visits. Whether he is close to home visiting the baseball culture of others, or affectionately writing about the mores and culture of El Salvador women, he is a sensitive observer. He is a thinking poet who has *positioned* himself in a way that has allowed his environments to compliment and feed his poetry.

First Light is divided into eight sections, each with its own music and purpose. I was particularly moved by section 4, "Mississippi." The reader senses and feels family, the writing spirit, the Mississippi sun and dust, the influence of the Black church and America's destruction of the unknown poet, bowillie. In two of the poems writes fondly of two fine writers, Ahmos Zu Bolton and Jerry Ward. Of Ahmos Zu Bolton he writes:

> I.
> in the house of zu
> the bible still works
> it runs well even without

batteries
all children born in this house
are taught early to recognize
the ways of the devil
they are constantly reminded
that "god don't like ugly"
in the house of zu
every child must learn
to read the mirror of life
before looking into it

II.

the poet ahmos was
the rebel spirit in the house of zu
he was the spirit that rejected god
and fell up into the hellfires of
the north
he is the spirit old folks say
took up writing because he could not see

III.

in deridder
there are more churches
than there are pews

In Miller's minimalist shorter works, he reminds me of
Lucille Clifton--compact, culturally to the bone and focused.
In his longer works he has a Sterling Brown ear, somewhat
blues-like without the repetition. However, he does have the
internal rhythms of the blues, and his poetry resonates in
Black idiom. The language and strength of the longer poems
are magical because he has discovered his voice. He has the
articulation of a lover, a lover of life, women, history, poetry
and the many people that inspire his work. His tributes to
W.E.B. DuBois, James Baldwin, C.L.R. James and Malcolm X,
tell us just as much about the poet as his subjects. He cares,
although conditionally. Like most Black men of his generation,
Malcolm X influenced his life and vision, and the poems
written of Malcolm are deeply felt and penetrating.

E. Ethelbert Miller is also uniquely a man's poet. The men he writes about and the conditions under which they live are memorable, and they cut without detour to the heart. He is also able to go in and out of his own environment to visit the lives of others. His poem on David Duke, Oscar Romero, Senor Rodriguez, the prison guard and the Bill Mazeroski poetry do what real poets are responsible for: hearing the heartbeat and feet of others.

Race personifies *First Light*, but it is not oppressive. He is not a *victim* writer; his work is quite liberating and yes, refreshing. This is important because he is such a good culturally conscious writer. This quality can be attributed to his highly developed conscience, and seriousness as a writer and an enlightened male sensibility. He does not fear the truths, a characteristic good poets can't do without. He comes to us in this volume full of hope and rich maturity. He shares the height of his experience and softness in, "Only Language Can Hold Us Together,"

> only language
> can hold us together
> i watch the women
> bead their hair
> each bead a word
> braids becoming
> sentences ...
> she never understood why
> no one ever understood the
> beauty of her hair ...

Miller is among the few African American writers producing today who has been nurtured and fully showered in the literature of his people. As the director of the African American Studies Resources Center at Howard University he has spent much of his adult life among our literature as well as the men and women who write it. As founder and organizer of the long running reading series *Ascension*, he has been responsible for highlighting the works of hundreds of writers--new and seasoned voices. He is truly committed to the literature, to writing, publishing and to a world where high literacy *can* be taken for granted. We have a difficult road to travel, but the "impossible" seems at hand with poets of this caliber.

Miller has populated his work with mothers, fathers, brothers, sisters and lovers who fight daily to be able to do simple things like drink clean water and sleep without gunshots interrupting their dreams. He takes instruction from Pablo Neruda, Margaret Walker, political prisoners and finds inspiration in the aloneness of Winnie Mandela. His work is highly political without becoming didactic as in "Tomorrow,"

> tomorrow
> i will take the
> journey back
> sail
> the middle passage
> it
> would be better
> to be packed
> like spoons again
> than
> to continue to
> live among
> knives and forks

This book will be memorable, read and re-read not because of political correctness, but due to the bone-fact that E. Ethelbert Miller is a word-musician. He is not practicing anymore. Each poem is its own melody, has its own life, which enables the reader to grow, to feel, to realize that real men do see and understand that life at its fullest requires reciprocity as in "poem for RV,"

> when you leave
> i realize how much
> my life needs air
> and how much loving

> you would be a reason
> for living   why are
> you so beautiful?
> why do i desire you as
> much as air?

First Light: New and Selected Poems is a mean collection of first rate poetry. Its silences are penetrating, its insights are liberating, its violence is quieting and its love is contagious. Read *First Light* and do something few people do in their life time, especially men, buy this poetry for a friend or two, and tell them that Haki put it on his must read list.

Haki R. Madhubuti

*Professor and Director of the Gwendolyn Brooks Center
Chicago State University*

E. Ethelbert Miller

PANAMA

Panama

in the early twenties
a boat brought
my father to America
his first impressions
were spoken in Spanish

years later when he
had forgotten the
language he could not
remember what he had

seen

Maintenance Man

with empty eyes
he lifts his
mop
out of
the bucket

water drips

cleaning
alone
in a tenement
hall

his
life
joins the
dust
in some
overlooked
corner

E. Ethelbert Miller

New York
(for marie)

in the pictures we are always
at the bronx zoo. you eat
ice cream while i watch
elephants. an attractive woman,
our mother stands by a fence
tightly holding her purse. this
is a deliberate and familiar pose,
one we will grow up with. we lived
on longwood avenue across from
p.s. 39. there were three locks
on our front door. you had several
boyfriends who were not permitted
to see you. once you were caught
kissing in the hall. i was in the
fourth grade, already convinced
i would marry you.

Bronx Bajans

we would take the train to brooklyn
leaving the bronx
down through harlem
out to prospect park
bergen street and franklin avenue
where everyone was cousin
aunt and uncle
where talk was about back home
and who died
and who got married
and who we were
we were always reminded
on sundays

E. Ethelbert Miller

The Things in Black Men's Closets

on the top shelf
of the closet
is the hat my father
wears on special occasions
it rests next to the large jar
he saves pennies in

his head is always bare
when i see him walking
in the street

i once sat in his bedroom
watching him search
between sweaters and suits
looking for something missing
a tie perhaps

then he stopped
and slowly walked to the closet
took the hat from the shelf

i sat on the bed
studying his back
waiting for him to turn
and tell me who died

Night

at some ungodly hour
her house shoes would scrape across
the wooden floor
as she moved from bedroom to kitchen
i would lie in my room and hear her
opening cabinets
washing dishes
placing a pot on the stove
then walking slowly back to where i was
to see how i was sleeping
to see if any blankets were on the floor

E. Ethelbert Miller

Jesus

on the day my grandfather died
his daughter the oldest
rushed to his house. there as his
body changed seasons she held
him in her arms, washed his body
with tears. when i was born
i almost died. my mother took me back
to the hospital. i was a blue baby
no one thought would live.
it was a miracle or so they
say. it was winter and the holiday
season. thanksgiving or christmas
i don't remember.

Fire

i am ten years old
and share a room with my brother.
at seventeen he dreams of becoming
a priest or monk. i am too young
to know the difference. in our room
the small bureau is an altar covered
with white cloth. two large candles
stand on each end. my fear of fire
begins in this room.

First Light

Growing Up

the day my mother
threw away my comic books
and encouraged me to read the bible
was the day i gave up being
a superhero and started to think
of miracles

this is how i came to love you
like moses looking over his
shoulder before he left that
mountain

E. Ethelbert Miller

1962: My Brother Richard Enters The Monastery

what do i remember? not much.
the trip to LaGuardia airport.
not too many colored people were flying
in those days. one had to walk out to the
airplane, i remember that. a number of us,
family and friends, had gone to see him off.
we laughed at Richard's head in the plane's
window. we were surprised we could see him and that
he could see us. we kept waving until the plane
turned around, slowly went down the runway, took
to the air and flew. my brother was gone. it would
be years before i understood that he could have
been gone forever. i think that evening my father
went to work as usual. my mother fell across the
bed in her room, crying. my sister told me to hush
and be quiet. i was the youngest, the baby, the other.
how was i to understand the lord's calling?

Faith: My Brother Richard Returns Home From The Monastery

i was not home
my mother, sister and i
had gone to the store
only my father was home

how happy he must have been
to open the door and see
his first born

to give your son
up to the lord is one thing
to receive him back is another

i would not have been surprised
if my father had lived the
rest of his life on his knees
i knew how grateful he was

faith is the meaning of love
between men

E. Ethelbert Miller

Questions Precede Faith

so many reasons
for leaving. which
one do i believe?
is it a choice
between god and family?
here i am the darker
brother. the only one.
i must keep an open
heart and an open
eye.

Men

my father and brother
have no wings
their legs are short
and cannot reach the ground

when i left home
i left walking on my head
i decided i would give birth
to a leopard

i stopped at the place
where the river disappears
into the sky

those of us who are birds
envy the leopard
even the strange ones
who call themselves men
hide inside their shells

E. Ethelbert Miller

Bronx Sketches

I

in the bronx
between beck and kelly
streets
alberto once
believed to be
the cisco kid
filled his watergun
with pee
and shot our heads in

we smelled bad
for days but did
not die
II
once an old white
musician
who played the
accordion came to
the alley behind
our building

he played for coins
his head
became the target
for our garbage
when we found
we couldn't latin
to his sound

A South Bronx Sketch

St. Mary's Park
was known
for rapes
robberies
even hangings

once Bob and I
saw a whole team
of Puerto Ricans
play stickball
with someone's head

the game ended
when their power
hitter cracked the
skull open

Bob and I
slid home fast
we never did
congratulate
the winners

E. Ethelbert Miller

Separation Demands That All Things Be Reduced To Pieces

the table is glass

you sit
resting your head

in the room
almost everything
is broken

i turn from
the window and move
quietly towards you

i smash my fist
into your skull

the sound is sharp

your head
like an antique vase
rolls from the table

how will you explain
this to your mother?

Fingerprints On Your Arm

after dinner
we argue
you slam the door
in my face

i throw
a toy truck
against the wall
it leaves a mark
on the wall like
my fingerprints
on your arm

there is blood
in my eyes

twenty years
from now a
stranger will
walk into a
restaurant and
notice your
scars

that could be
the start of a
conversation

E. Ethelbert Miller

Michelle

I wanted to love you
without lust

but I am not the saint
I claimed to be
forgive me for taking
too much

maybe tomorrow
things will be different

it is unfortunate
that the sun does not
travel backwards

Iran

a few days before the taking
of hostages in iran
i obtain a divorce from my wife
i leave the courthouse blindfolded
although i cannot see
i know that another fanatic is out there
ready to terrorize me with love
i walk home quickly
fearful of the next explosion

The First Time
(for stb)

the
first time
we made love
i stayed awake
the entire night
watching you
sleep

the man
next door
kept clearing
his throat

E. Ethelbert Miller

October 31
(for june)

tonight i have flashes
of being the streaks of silver
in your hair

First Light
(for denise)

the cat opens the door to the bedroom
i see you sleeping alone
the covers hiding your face
it is a few hours before first light
today is mother's day
there is unfinished work on my desk
a few unpaid bills
i have been reading raymond carver
how does a man give birth to a poem?
with difficulty and great anticipation

E. Ethelbert Miller

Jasmine

on my desk is a small bottle
which once held perfume
inside is the cord that joined
my wife and daughter

it is strange that i keep it

my mother kept my brother's
sixth finger in a jar stuffed
with cotton

one night i found it
while secretly searching
for cookies hidden in a drawer
filled with underwear
why do we keep things that are not ours?

in another land
an old woman would take this cord
and place it in the earth

tomorrow when my daughter becomes a woman
i will give her this small bottle
filled with the beginnings of herself

on that day she will hold love
in her hands

The Second Child
(for nyere-gibran)

in sports they say it's difficult
to repeat, to win, to gain a championship
two consecutive years; so it is with children,
the difference, the new season, the second child.

each beginning finds a newborn, a rookie
struggling to learn the lessons of spring,
a time of hope and expectations, of fingers
gripping and pulling things to mouth.

E. Ethelbert Miller

The Vase

sleep shatters
i hear the sound
of something crashing
in the next room
i know my favorite
vase is broken
i always knew the cat
would knock it down
so there is no anger
inside me this morning
only disappointment

another wedding gift
has broken
something once so
beautiful

i rise
from the bed
where my wife
sleeps unaware
of what has
happened

she has kept
our vows

New York
(for Enid)

in the 1940's
my mother worked in the garment district
of new york. she did piecework,
getting paid by the rhinestones she sewed
on dresses and skirts.
in the middle of the night
i change my daughter's pajamas in the dark.
my hands peeling the wet clothes from her small
body. this is done without wearing glasses.
my skill amazes me. i lead my daughter
to the bathroom, there i find a washcloth and
wipe away the smell of urine. she stands naked
in the center of a brown rug. my hands moving
quickly are the hands of my mother.

Enid At 70

once the world was as large as your breasts
shelter and safety were in your arms
now i seek protection and the world turns away
i think of lincoln walking alone in the white house
a civil war outside and young men embracing death
you are my mother a widow at seventy

E. Ethelbert Miller

Hotel

i think of the last
time i made love to my wife.
it was our wedding night
ten years ago. we were in a
hotel near georgetown.
before we undressed she left
the room. she went down the
hall to find ice to cool the
champagne. while she was away
the telephone rang. a woman i
was in love with called to
congratulate me. we talked for
a minute and then she was gone.
we made love like that once. my
wife came back into the room
smiling. she saw the look on
my face.

40 Harrison Street

down the hall of the seventeenth floor
we walk to the apartment
marie has the keys and i follow behind
carrying blue luggage
to neighbors we resemble our mother and
father returning from the movies
two keys unlock the door
opening a moment of silence

the small apartment is like a plant
in need of water
i place the blue bag by the door
marie turns on the kitchen light
our father died two days ago
the bedroom remains dark
our mother is resting in a hospital uptown

i stand in the middle of the small living
room filled with old furniture, my parent's
wedding gifts from the early forties
i walk to the piano and wish i could
remember how to play

E. Ethelbert Miller

Family Pictures
(for denise)

we wake up early
shower separately
i dress in the bathroom
while you look for the iron
in the kitchen closet
for breakfast you have coffee
with light cream
i take chinese tea with lemon
you brush your hair in the mirror
place powder and lipstick on your face
i find the belt for my pants

we clean the house before we leave
i empty the trash
give the cat fresh litter
you wash the four dishes and the one
cup left in the sink

i stop to watch the plants hanging
in the window
i count the dead leaves

we have lived together for three weeks
sharing the space within each other
i write in the last pages of my diary
outside the cars move in different
directions
family pictures on the bookshelf
you smile and remind me of what day it is

Art Is A Long Way From This Moment

if i didn't make up these poems
would you believe my life
the emptiness so rich it overflows
with loneliness   who are you
but a woman who walks inside her
own mystery   whose love is so
external it describes only gestures
you are the dream that did not last
the night   i am the man whose face
you will remember when your husband
returns from his affairs   let my
poems console you   here is the
pain i felt when you left

E. Ethelbert Miller

*BILL MAZEROSKI RETURNS
HOME FROM THE WORLD SERIES*

The Kid

about the second month of the season
we start catching word about the kid
talk about strikeouts and shutouts
how his curve breaks and his fastball smokes
frank and i were driving trucks up in the mountains
listening to the games
betting our wages and drinking beer
we get the newspapers each morning and check the standings
frank is a giants fan
been that way since the day willie mays broke in
that was the same year his father died
in an accident on the highway three days before christmas
sometimes when we ain't talking about baseball
frank will talk about his father
talk about him the way some folks be talking about the kid

The Trade

the first time i put on a different uniform
i think about marilyn and our divorce, the year
i was trying to win a second batting title and anything
that came my way i couldn't miss. i was comfortable at
the plate and at home. so how could she leave knowing
so much about me? minor league records, walks, times hit
by a pitch, even my superstitions like wearing the same
socks until i went hitless in a game or sleeping only
on my left side during the month of august. i love
marilyn with the same feeling i get when i see a ball
bouncing off the wall, the centerfielder backing up the
play with a young arm as strong as accurate as any in the
league. the shortstop, the cutoff man waiting on the edge
of the grass. my spikes softly, quickly touching the inside
of second as something unknown inside decides to stretch a
double into a triple, sending my arms and legs forward
as smooth as anything invented by god. i hit the bag standing
and my lungs echo the ball coming to rest inside the third
baseman's glove. now suddenly the trade after ten years
with the same team. i find a new insignia and letters scrawled
across my chest, a sign of ownership and no comfort for a slave
or player of this game. i think of marilyn packing her clothes
or bringing the kids to see me during the early days of
separation. once we argued in the parking lot after a game
and a fan interrupted us for an autograph. we laughed
and went home together and made love and i thought
i would have a fourth chance. but marilyn came out of the
bathroom drying tears from her body
and she stood there as naked and helpless as the rookie
phil bostic the day they sent him to the minors and he knew
he was never coming back.

E. Ethelbert Miller

Playoffs

while i watch the playoffs
you use my phone to call
some other man

you stay until
the fifth inning
then you say you have
to leave

i watch you exit
like a pitcher heading
for the showers

somewhere someone
is keeping score

you perfect your game
with each man

love is the best curve
a woman can throw

Twilight

lou only stepped on the foul line
after he had decided to remove a pitcher
i knew he was going to keep me in
so i turned my back to the plate
stared at the runner on second
a spanish kid just down from spokane
he looks at me with pity
then spits into the dust around his spikes
lou's hand touches my back pocket
like a woman telling a friend to go ahead
i'm right behind you

tough break he mumbles
and al the catcher comes up alongside
my pitching arm
whistling a song that was a hit a few
years ago
catchers never talk when you've lost it
they keep calling their game and staring
at the dugout for someone to make a change
al was good at never letting you know

lou turns and heads back to the dugout
everything he said leaves a bad taste
in my mouth
the umpire sweeps the plate
the next batter steps into the box
al punches the dark spot of his glove
checks his mask and bends his knees

i stand on the mound waiting for the sign
twilight and my hand grips the ball the way
my father held my shoulders the day he said
he had to leave

E. Ethelbert Miller

Helen

sometimes after someone has hit a foul
the umpire will toss a new ball back to the pitcher
the pitcher will catch it   look at it   rub it
then toss it back and ask that umpire for a new ball
just the other night i'm making love to helen
and it feels strange
helen got her eyes all closed
she's squirming and moaning
but you can tell she's thinking about someone else
i run my fingers down her back like i'm tracing
the seams on a ball

Helen & Martha

after i got his third letter
i decided not to write
didn't know what to say or not say
went by the house yesterday and saw his wife and kid
ask if she heard from him
"no he ain't wrote since he left" she said
and i'm sittin by the kitchen table playin with the kid
thinkin about my three letters
and why i got them and she ain't
she his wife and me i don't know what i am
men always give me problems and other people men
well they give me headaches
problems and headaches is like water in your basement
reachin for the first floor
since i come to blue mountain
i don't think about nothin but keeping my own business
and believe me somebody's man
ain't what i like to poke my nose into

Martha & Helen

she got the body i once had
the kind men look for in magazines
i know why he be chasin after her
and why she always here playin
with my kid like she tryin to
make up for what she done or what
she's thinkin about doin
i know all his lies and i'm
learnin hers   i bet she got a
couple of letters already
he tryin to keep her warm
like a cup of coffee he can
come back to

E. Ethelbert Miller

Bill Mazeroski Returns Home From The World Series

when i was a kid
i told my old man
that i would make a name for myself
like walter next door who had a hit
record on the radio for two weeks
and then enlisted and got himself shot

i want people to forget eisenhower
i want them to remember my swing
the way i touched third and headed
home to every fan in the world

On Killing Myself Without First Saying Hello

in the middle of writing this
i have a strong desire
to be a relief pitcher
in a baseball game
it doesn't matter for whom
or what's the score
i want to see how my curve breaks
i want to know if i can still bring it
without having my arm
bend like a broken wing
the poem lifeless
as it sails over a fence

E. Ethelbert Miller

GROW YOUR OWN CHINESE VEGETABLES

Grow Your Own Chinese Vegetables

i suffer slowly now
pain without swelling
evenings without horizons
the dog sits by the door
too tired to walk itself
plants hang from windows
your photograph walks
across the room
and picks out another record
in the kitchen i teach myself
to grow chinese vegetables
across the street
the bus stop practices
meditation
rosa parks laughs at willie mays
losing his cap
it's terrible how these things
happen

Sunrise

what is memory but
the sunrise each day.
how could i forget you
and embrace so much
darkness?

E. Ethelbert Miller

Personal #1, 1975

the unmanned satellite
streaking through the
emptiness of space
catches only the distant
light of stars on its
metallic skin

Personal #2, 1975

in
search
of an
executioner

I walk
unprotected
down alleys
a

sacrifice
for some
junkie god

E. Ethelbert Miller

Personal #1976

all alone
i am saigon

turning to communism

the embassy of my soul
invaded
helicopters like women
lift off and depart

days become dominoes

i surrender to my own war

Marathon

it's a strange time which finds me jogging
in early morning
the deadness of sleep alive in this world
the empty parks filled with unloved strangers
buildings grey with solitude
now near the end of another decade
i am witness to the loss of my twenties
a promise invisible
i run without purpose
far from the north star
i run with the sound of barking dogs closing in
i have lost count of the miles
i am older and nothing much matters
or has changed

E. Ethelbert Miller

Poem

let me die at 33
like john reed
a witness to revolution
& his own turbulence
i want to be the man
you know by name & reputation
not by touch

The Kneelers

the old
prayers
answered
we kneelers
now stand
and walk away
the new
prayers
will
bring us
back

E. Ethelbert Miller

Baptism

spring comes like a deacon with a bible
i feel the heat of the sun on my back
the river not far ahead
i think about the baptism
what it means
i find myself walking to the water
my soul singing about salvation
is this what my mother wanted all these years?
hallelujah someone shouts
take me to the water
jesus is my friend
i am alone and there are too many believers
who will lead me home in the morning?

Ethelbert By The Lake

he sits in a chair
staring at the water
thinking of poems
setting some free
to drift

E. Ethelbert Miller

Path

holy
is
the
man
who
walks
alone

Untitled

if i must suffer and live alone
in the ruins of some lost or forgotten city
let it be one that has known
the civilization of your love

E. Ethelbert Miller

MISSISSIPPI

Only Language Can Hold Us Together

only language
can hold us together

i watch the women
bead their hair
each bead a word

braids becoming
sentences

she would
never comb her hair
it was always wild

like new poetry
it was difficult
to understand

she would enter
rooms where old women
would stare & mumble
& bold ones would say

"where's her mother"

she never understood why
no one ever understood the
beauty of her hair

like free verse
so natural as conversation
so flowing like the french

or spanish she heard or
overheard she thought she knew

"i want to go to
mozambique" she said one day

combing her hair
finding the proper beads
after so long

"i want to go to
mozambique" she said

twisting her hair
into shape the way her
grandmother made quilts
each part separated &
plaited

"i want to go to
mozambique or zimbabwe
or someplace like luanda

i need to do something
about my hair

if only i could
remember

the words
to the language
that keeps
breaking in my
hands"

E. Ethelbert Miller

Deridder: The Southern Sequence
To Southern Spirit

on ollie street
in deridder louisiana
13 spirits live in the house of zu

I.

in the house of zu
the bible still works
it runs well even without
batteries

all children born in this house
are taught early to recognize
the ways of the devil

they are constantly reminded
that "god don't like ugly"

in the house of zu
every child must learn
to read the mirror of life
before looking into it

II.

the poet ahmos was
the rebel spirit in the house of zu

he was the spirit that rejected god
and fell up into the hellfires of
the north

he is the spirit old folks say
took up writing because he could not see

III.

> in deridder
> there are more churches
> than there are pews

IV.

> russell chew
> is the preacher for
> the church of the living god
>
> a slender man
> he took it upon himself
> not to let evil by

V.

> when the poet ahmos
> came home to deridder
> his mother met him at the door
>
> she gave him a strange look
> and without a kiss
> said in a stranger's voice
>
> "I'll tell you right now son
> there ain't gonna be no
> curses in my home
>
> make sure when you come in
> that you leave dem poems
> at the door"

VI.

> deridder is a dry town

E. Ethelbert Miller

some folks like it
that way

others are into bootlegging

in the last election
to decide to change the
deridder law

the god-fearing people
fixed the ballots
by having dead people
vote

"dead people don't
care too much about
changing things"

someone said

VII.

mrs. clay
lives next door to
russell chew

old
her face seems
no longer to age

her features speak
of indian blood

but her
grandchildren
are the only tribe
she claims

VIII.

people on ollie street
have memories that remember
old things

they can remember the small ahmos
before he picked up his pen

they can remember the young chew
before he carried the cross

both kids always dreamed
of leaving deridder

their dreams always tried
to escape the bars of ollie street

ollie street
is two blocks long

with two dead ends

IX.

mrs. clay
once told russell chew
that there was more
to religion than
just praying

chew responded by saying

"until folks stop running
away from jesus
it's good to keep them on
their knees"

E. Ethelbert Miller

X.

in deridder
the same things
come and go

each day brings
the same

the bible
is read

before
sunrise

and

after
sunset

Mississippi

death surrounds itself with the living
i watch them take the body from the house
i'm a young kid maybe five years old
the whole thing makes no sense to me
i hear my father say
      lord jesus what she go and do this for
i watch him walk out the backdoor of the house
i watch him walk around the garden
kick the dirt
stare at the flowers
& shake his head shake his head
he shakes his head all night long

yazoo
jackson
vicksburg
we must have family in almost every city
i spent more time traveling than growing up
guess that's why i'm still shorter than my old man
he don't like to stay in one place much
he tell me
soon as people get to know your last name
seem like they want to call you by your first
boy   if someone ask you your name
tell them to call you mississippi
not sippi or sip but mississippi

how many colored folks you know name mississippi

none see

now you can find a whole lot of folks whose

E. Ethelbert Miller

name is canada
just like you can find 53 people in any phone book
whose name is booker t. washington

your mother she was a smart woman
gave you a good name
not one of them abolitionist names

what you look like with a name like
john brown or william lloyd garrison
that don't have no class

your mother she named you after the river
cause of its beauty and mystery
just like my mother named me nevada
cause she didn't know where it was

The Last Days of BoWillie
(for jerry ward)

we sat out on the porch
tired from the long trip
the ride down from the north
cold beer rested at our feet
water from the icebucket dripping
from the cans like it would a young
dog's tongue
from off the road
dust occasionally climbed the three steps of the porch
strutted past the four of us
blew quietly beneath the door and found
a cool spot under bojava's couch
jerry took a turn at his pipe
now and then puffed smoke at the full moon
i stared at the fireflies off in the distance
something i had not done or seen since maybe
the time i was seven or eight
shirley had the corner of the porch to herself
a bag of nuts in her lap
at times only a cracking sound could be heard among the four
of us then the sipping from a can
a cough
bojava got up first
walked to the front of the porch
stretched and then gave a good spit into the dark
by the way he stood looking at nothing
we knew he would talk
sooner or later

E. Ethelbert Miller

his words came slowly
like he was tasting each one
holding them back for the last bit of juice
he spat again
any of you remember bowillie?
causing a small explosion
bojava knew he had our attention
i said yeah
i think so
you mean bowillie the poet?
yeah
bojava spoke without turning around
there is no need for us to look at each other
our skulls already divide the landscapes of north and south
bojava speaks
his words like winter in december
do you remember when they hung him?
the three of us remained quiet
we knew he was speaking to the spirit in us
the fireflies made small sparks in the woods
shirley brought the silence to an end
by reaching in her bag for another nut
she cracked this one in her hand
that man
bowillie was a rootdoctor
a conjure man
a trickster
            he learned his magic on a chain gang in galveston
taught thieves and murderers the blue songs of their fathers
he broke rocks that no man dare touch
no bars could hold him to this earth

no one spot could claim his shadow
when he escaped to washington
it was during the rise of the klan
even the sky was on fire
he once called the place demon city
a mecca for vampires
he rode the subway searching for cave drawings
he was sure he would find
a sign of evidence that this city
this land was not the property
of its owners but instead belonged to its slaves
bojava turned and looked at us
he was soft spoken but now his voice rose
bowillie destroyed their monuments
all of them
no one knew how
but he destroyed the museums
the government buildings/everything
when they caught him it was too late
washington is now filled with ghosts
politicians who make laws
supreme court judges who wear white robes instead of black
the day they hung bowillie
i saw birds fall from the sky
i saw leaves on trees turn red
jerry watched the dust coming up from down the road
i sat listening to my heart beat in my throat
shirley closed her bag of nuts
bojava sat back down
the beer   still cold at his feet

E. Ethelbert Miller

Untitled

when
you're
small

white
folks
always

want
to touch
your head

for
good
luck

Airport: A Takeoff On A Poem

sitting in the airport
for about two hours
i finally landed a conversation
with an old white lady who looked
mulatto
she asked me if i was a student
at the university
i told her no
she asked me what i did
i told her i wrote poetry
she asked me what i wanted to do
i told her i had always
wanted to kill a large number of people
i told her of my desire to climb into
clocktowers and be a sniper
i told her that i had missed the draft
and was too proud to enlist
i told her about all the audie murphy
films i had ever seen
i told her that i was the type
that carried bombs inside luggage
when making short trips
i watched the old mulatto lady
turn white
there was no mistaking it now
she was a white lady and i...

well i have been sitting in this
airport for over two hours more
listening to the soft ticking sounds
coming from the case i carry my poems in

E. Ethelbert Miller

Untitled

we are all
black poets
at night

Incantation
(for jonetta)

let all poems speak and address themselves
let each phrase like hair on a head
comb itself back madame walker style
let the love poems wear gardenias
let the political poems wear suits the way muslims did
during the days of elijah
let the poems be fruitful and multiply

E. Ethelbert Miller

A DEATH IN THE FAMILY

Elizabeth Keckley: 30 Years A Slave And 4 Years In The White House

tall man lincoln looking out the windows
of this white house. i wonder what he's
thinking. the war not far from here. men
dying. death trying to get indoors. i rise
before his wife asks for anything. all the
dresses i make, everything i touch is black.
sometimes i can't tell the difference between
war and slavery. i do my work and only forget
what i don't care to remember. lincoln is not
well, he looks old. his wife calls his name
every night. it's me who holds her hand after
he leaves. she talks to me like i'm a ghost
and not a colored woman.

W.E.B. DuBois

in philadelphia
i studied the negro
i knew everything
about him

in atlanta
i lost my first
born

what do i know
about myself?
there is so
much to learn

Malcolm X, August 1952

i suppose i should be
grateful to the white man
letting me out. where can
a black man in america go?
i stand with the prison in
my shadow. elijah muhammad
teaches us that we are not
thieves. we are the lost ones
who have been stolen.

allah bless my tongue as it
prepares to heal. there are
so many who are in need of
the message. i feel this
country changing. the cross
no longer ours to bear.

Malcolm X, 1964

there are so many muslims
in the world. so many. all colors.
i am one, trying to be one. there
is so much to see and learn. once
i submitted to my own ignorance.
once i submitted to a man i believed
was divine. now a new journey begins
with myself. i make the hajj. i
embrace my soul. there is no god but
allah.

E. Ethelbert Miller

Malcolm X, February 1965

i will die this month. how
i do not know. still there
is much work to be done. i
am afraid not for myself but
for betty and the girls. some
nights i stay awake looking
out the window, a gun in my
hand. i know how cruel people
can be. i have known hatred and
blindness. there are brothers
waiting to do me harm. i will
die for them. i will love them
as only i can. may allah be my
witness.

A Death In The Family

it was dinky's father
mr. skinner who told my mother
that someone shot malcolm x

malcolm x?
my mother repeated
wasn't he the one who looked
so much like our own sonny boy?

E. Ethelbert Miller

Baldwin

you lie in bed listening,
waiting, fearing the moment
your father returns home. you
listen to voices talking in the
next room and wonder why you are
still afraid of the dark. his voice
in the other room you would love to
kiss. you cannot see your face in the
dark but the blackness is there, like
his back. if only he would
open the door and look at you. maybe
the light would be in his eyes,
his voice.

Not Slavery But South Africa
(for cecelie)

sometimes
when i think
about south africa
i imagine myself
to be an escaped slave
living in canada
during the 1850's
wondering about things
in america

the distance
between
oppression & freedom
is not measured by time
or separated by the borders
of countries

the distance
between
oppression & freedom
is measured by our willingness
to fight & destroy our fears

to understand
the distance
already travelled

E. Ethelbert Miller

C.L.R. James
(for p. buhle)

i sit next
to the old man
surrounded in
his bed by books
the television
is on but he
has already
started asking
questions

i try to
remember
this moment
for the rest
of my life

i let
everything
else become
history

ATLANTIC CITY

Atlantic City

we drove north to new jersey.
we had our friend carla's car. aisha's
brother had been killed in newark. shot
five times in the head. she talked
about her family while i drove. i don't
like any of them, she said. i don't know
why i'm going to the funeral. maybe we
should go to atlantic city, she joked.
i thought it was a good idea. she never
told me her brother's name. it didn't
matter. life is luck, a name nothing but
chance.

Rafael

the day
rafael was pushed
from the roof we knew
he was different. we knew
he could die and we could
live. live to laugh at him
begging for his life. how
stupid he looked, handsome
face and all. what a pity
to be so beautiful and not
be able to fly.

After She Told Me This Her Husband Killed The Kids

trapped. you ask how i feel or how i felt. trapped.

well that's the only word i can

find that would capture or define

what it is i can't explain.

three years maybe more, i forget unless i count the jobs.

the part-time ones and the night-time ones.

the ones i'm ashamed of and the ones i rather not recall.

i did alright by myself with

three kids, the youngest not too smart

and the oldest, a girl and getting prettier everyday.

i think she knows more than i did or more than i know now.

i lose count of days and the nights i subtract from where i ache,

the place where a man is supposed to be.

i started writing to him in prison when he didn't come home,

and when he returned home i didn't know him.

i once knew his eyes. i fell in love with his eyes,

now i'm afraid of this man with the look, the glance, the stare

too strange to forget. i'm afraid he will tear into me and open

my insides and i'll bleed leaving the sound of a heart beating

in search of a vacancy for love. trapped. it's the only word i

can think of. the kids need this and they need that and i cook,

clean, wash and everything i would give away for romance,

for music, for happiness tonight,

or a moment when we kiss like this,

and i fly into the air.

when we kiss like this and i fly into

the air.

E. Ethelbert Miller

Bighead & Snotnose

they come around
the corner speeding in their cars
their sirens panting and their guns
dangling as they step into our world
pushing us back into nowhere
and nowhere left to hide our faces
and now our names faceless as we stare
at their whiteness and dark blue mysteries
filled with law resting heavy in the air

bighead and snotnose
freeze like basketball stars
going to the hoop
their bodies suspending over history
as they pump and fake and double fake
and dare laws to stop their lives
on a corner where they lean
as cool as gravity
pulling their sneakers
back to earth

Lorton

it is 16 miles out to lorton
where the hills catch virginia sunlight
and breaks things into many colors
where horses graze behind wire fences
and clothes dry behind small homes and
where the road twists and turns and finally bends
there are gates and walls and guards and guns
and the silence where the sunlight
passes through the prison is where the
men divide men and give some numbers

E. Ethelbert Miller

Prison

it's my duty to stand by the first
door, the last door depending on
which way you're going. you learn
to read faces, know who's scared
and who's tough. some have the look
of death while others don't have
nothing. their faces appear to be
stuck on red, like a light on a
corner. tonight i came home early
and told my wife once again about
the boys, how the colored don't
seem to show their age. maybe someone
catching them younger she says. she
brings me a beer that i've been
saving for a moment like this. i open
it and give her a sip. she puts her
hand on my chest and tells me to
forget about work. i reach over her
and turn off the light.

Rape

i n
dark alleys
the beauty
of women
is violated

lust runs
uncontrolled
through
the pants
of men

E. Ethelbert Miller

Duke

no job
sleeping in the backseat of a car
moving from town to town
that's how it starts
that's how it begins
here in louisiana
where the money
once was like oil
slick and black

now the dirt is dust
the hunting is gone
and the river doesn't answer
when you call

so what can i tell you about david duke
except that he knows these parts, these people
and the inside of their prayers
papers say he a racist but who ain't these days
colored ain't no different from the whites
in that regards...
i knew his daddy and both of them come from
small towns no bigger than this one
start right here with some of my best friends
beer drinking, blue jean wearing, dixie hummin
folks like myself

that's why i voted for him
i took him by his word
and his word was white folks need to
organize before colored folks do

you take a man by his word
and sometimes it's as good
as your own hand in your pocket

now you know what i do?
i pick politicians mostly by their wives
if she look like she's been cheated on
i can tell at them rallies and press conferences
any man cheat on his wife
will do anything to deny it
but you know if he lie to his wife
he just might be one of the boys
i don't mind that that's politics
that's how the system works

i don't confess to messing with
any colored gals but i know a few
fellas who have
but it wasn't nothin
just a little fun on a friday night

like chasing those civil righters
those northern boys and jews

in the old days we had a lot of fun
and the colored kids the little ones
knew how to laugh, beg for money, shine
shoes and dance

now if you put some of these grown-up boys
in a voting booth there's no telling
what they'll do

E. Ethelbert Miller

i need a job just as much as my wife
needs love
you know what i'm talking about?

the first time i heard david duke
speak i knew things were getting better
i'm tired of someone putting words in
the mouths of politicians

it's about time a white man speak the truth
if you don't want to hear the truth
then you don't know what the truth is

i love this country
this louisiana
this place where good food is just
waiting to be fixed
and the stars shine every night
like children when you give them sweets

don't let me ever catch the river running
the wrong way
i don't know what i do
what can a man believe in if things change?
david duke he's alright
he talks the way i talk
and this is louisiana
you a stranger if you don't know it

A Walk In The Daytime Is Just As Dangerous As A Walk In The Night

a simple dirt road
surrounded by all these mountains
trees and lakes
does not offer calmness
to my soul or mind
even here in upstate new york
the stillness drives a fear
through my heart like mississippi
or history and i cannot walk
without hearing the barking of dogs
or the yell from some redneck
screaming "there he goes"
i try to accept all these things
as irrational fears that
i should enjoy this time in the
country to relax and be at peace
with myself and i am happy
to be out walking in the morning
on this road which runs into
route 28 near eagle lake
not far from the small town
where i plan to purchase stamps
and postcards and while
i'm walking along the highway
feeling good about the weather
and thinking about nothing in particular
two vans filled with people
speed by and disturb the quiet and call me

E. Ethelbert Miller

"nigger"

and the peaceful walk is no more
and in the midst of all this
beautiful scenery i become a woman
on a dark city street vulnerable
to any man's attack
it is not yet mid-afternoon
but the virginity of my blackness
has been raped
and this is no longer
a simple walk into town
this is like every walk i have taken
in my life wherever and whenever
i have been alone and my fears are
as real as this dirt beneath
my feet

EL SALVADOR

Tomorrow

tomorrow
i will take the
journey back
sail
the
middle passage
it
would be better
to be packed
like spoons again
than
to continue to
live among
knives and forks

Untitled

where are the love poems for dictators
i sit on a stool in a small room
no windows
i can touch walls without moving my arms
the smell of myself eats the last slice of air
in this prison
the food is terrible
it is a tasteless horror
in the next cell antonio weeps
his body already crushed by a thousand burns
at night i whisper poetry through the cracks
in the wall
my words like women kiss his eyes

E. Ethelbert Miller

Juan

i meet juan
at the outskirts
of our village
we say nothing
walk to the water
where boats sleep
stuck in sand
we push one forward
into the smells of morning
check our nets
as the sun looks through
the openings in heaven

Señor Rodriguez

the old truck creaks
to the side of the road
victor the driver says we have to walk
the last miles to the fields
señor rodriguez refused to fix the truck again
he is an old man who sleeps with his money
now that his wife is dead
there are 12 men in victor's truck
another 30 somewhere in the dust ahead
we all carry machetes
the inside of our hands hard like the earth
we live on
our shirts hang from our chests like leaves too
tired to fall
i listen to victor curse the truck
the way i do the sun and señor rodriguez
in the middle of the afternoon
when sweat runs like rivers down the muscles
of my back and i have only prayers
to count the hours

E. Ethelbert Miller

What The Women Told Me

the women were making clay bowls
afterwards they washed their hands
went indoors to find their shawls

they
say

when hector was killed
when the soldiers decided to cut
his stomach open for fun
two things happened even stranger
than the war

first

a hundred doves flew from the opening
in his body
each dove taking a drop of hector's blood

and
then (yes the women say this is true)

hector opened his eyes
after his stomach had been opened
from his eyes grew flowers and songs

the soldiers
reloaded their guns
took aim and did not miss

Juanita

when she was small
she wore the lipstick of her mother
face made older with powder
like the pictures of movie stars
cut from magazines
the blonde ones she taped on the wall
next to jesus

E. Ethelbert Miller

Soldier

i didn't want to be a farmer
like my father or brothers
so i became a soldier
it was difficult but i did it
i was skinny when i started my training
my captain told me
after a few killings
i would put on weight

El Salvador

the soldiers march through the streets
like the beads of my mother's rosary
i count them
i lose count
i count again
i am not afraid of dying
so much death i have seen
the grass red
the flowers red
the rivers the color of blood
there are fingers where leaves once floated
there are flies fasting from too much flesh
when peace returns
this land will be filled with farmers not funerals
i swear it
mother of god

E. Ethelbert Miller

She Wore A Red Dress

in salvador
there is talk of elections
but rumors travel like death squads
the shadow on the corner is not a man

in the morning
i see bodies
lying on the ground
like discarded bottles and cans

in the afternoon
everything is normal
streets are crowded
children return from school
mothers shop
young girls flirt
with legs miraculously
scarless

in salvador
i am constantly
looking over my shoulder

it has nothing
to do with beauty

Francisco

sometimes there is no body to bury
no coffin to carry
people disappear
made invisible
like francisco
who was sleeping in his bed
the night someone stole him
from his dreams

E. Ethelbert Miller

I Am The Land: A Poem
In Memory of Oscar Romero

I am the land.
I am the grass growing.
I am the trees.
I am the wind, the voice calling.
I am the poor.
I am the hungry.

The doors of the church are open
as wide as the heart of a man.
In times of trouble
here is a rock, here is a hand.

God knows the meaning of our prayers.
I have asked our government to listen.
God is not dead
and I will never die.

I am the land.
I am the grass growing.
I am the trees.
I am the wind, the voice calling.
I am the poor.
I am the hungry.

He who is resurrected is revolutionary.
He who is resurrected believes in peace.
This is the meaning of light.
This is the meaning of love.

The souls of my people are the pages of history.
The people of El Salvador are the people of the world.

I am Oscar Romero, a humble servant.
I am the land.
I am all the people who have no land.
I am the grass growing.
I am all the children who have been murdered.
I am the trees.
I am the priests, the nuns, the believers.
I am the wind, the voice calling.
I am the poets who will sing forever.
I am the poor.
I am the dreamer whose dreams overflow with hope.
I am the hungry.
I am the people.
I am Oscar Romero.

E. Ethelbert Miller

So You Ask About Nicaragua

several days after somoza fled
i left the house of a friend and
went outside to take pictures of the stars
it was the first time i noticed them

After The Generals

there are new slogans in the air & on the walls
i watch my mother at work in the kitchen
she is learning slowly how to read
slowly stumbling out of the past
now & then she rests her head on the table
the pages of her notebook filled with promises
my mother can spell and read so many words
she tries to read the newspaper everyday
& everyday she has questions

how long will this revolution be?
when will we have more food?
why was manuel killed?
were not things better under the generals?

questions
& more questions
& questions i cannot answer

what do i tell my mother
a woman with so few tomorrows

how much forgiveness remains in her heart
& after the rule of generals
what is left to forgive

E. Ethelbert Miller

When Allende Was Alive

looking through the window of my country
i do not see myself outside
i trace the outline of my breath against glass
the cold enters my fingers

when allende was alive
i could open this window
look out across chile from my home in
santiago

there were no curtains to hide dreams
it was a time of hope

a time to press democracy against my lips
& hold her like a lover

Roberto

in chile
maria
holds
roberto
in her hands
in her hand
a photograph

gone
is the
laughter
& the smile
of our friend

when
i ask
the authorities
about roberto
they shrug
their shoulders
they say
they have
not seen him

they ask
is he
missing

between
life & death
there are only
pictures

E. Ethelbert Miller

There Is A Place Where The Sea Goes When It Is Tired

last week we marched to the square
to protest the shortage of food
we were women not politicians
we were mothers not communists
we were thousands not hundreds

it made no difference

bayonets and blood
they beat us
clubbed us
opened our stomachs
with knives

they told us

do not worry
about food

the dead do not starve

Thriller

it's close to midnight
& america wonders why michael jackson
wears one glove
while in argentina jews are missing
& the coast of nicaragua
is surrounded by mines

america
falls in love with michael jackson
& no one is curious
about CIA involvement in central
america

michael jackson turns into a monster
& ronald reagan becomes teddy roosevelt
the whole western hemisphere
is westside story
tonight
maybe for katherine hepburn
& the girls in the balcony
we should stop & examine history
before it's too late

america remove your sunglasses

E. Ethelbert Miller

Spanish Conversation

in cuba
a dark-skinned woman asks me
if i'm from angola
i try to explain in the no spanish i know
that i am american

she finds this difficult to believe
at times i do too

Postcards From Miami

from the restaurant we could see
the hotel that survived the earthquake
further proof that this country
needed us what could one buy now
except cheap jewelry and the latest
fashions from eastern europe some
of us who stayed after the revolution
slept with postcard pictures of miami
over our heads   there are no clubs and
the movies come from cuba   still we meet
in the afternoon to drink and remember
the good days   the beer is warm and the
wine expensive the good stuff was gone
long ago like lucille ball we try to
laugh and convince ourselves that life
too is filled with reruns

E. Ethelbert Miller

America

so many of us in exile
our own children
request we speak english

on cold nights
the kitchen becomes
heated with talk
about politics

in a corner
a blanket almost
covers the face
of josé

three days old
he has already
lived longer
than his two
sisters

things are
better now

this new country
is not a grave

Solidarity

(for roberto vargas)

when trees bend funny and out of shape
when lightblue skies turn blueblack grey
hungry winds will
knock behind the bellycaves
of coffee colored strangers
and hurricanes will come
and speak no english

Port-Au-Prince

inside the car
françois and i
could see the light
coming from the
cigarette michele
duvalier was smoking
her husband
declared president
for life looked like
a fat chauffeur
sitting behind the
wheel

françois
and i smiled

the small
procession of cars
slipping past us
in the dark

we did not know
that a few miles
away people were
already celebrating
nor could we see
joy on the faces
of the men who ran
holding knives and
sticks to the place
where papa doc

was buried
tonight even
ghosts will die
as françois and i
walk barefoot
to the center
of port-au-prince

E. Ethelbert Miller

Bronx Snapshot

andre's father
was from Haiti

he was a happy man
who kept a jar
of white people
in his window

kept them in a
milk of magnesia
bottle

Poem #1

if i had a pass
i could watch the
sunset in johannesburg
instead i ride the crowded
train
the hot smell of my brothers
mixing with the dust
the coming blackness of the
night
moving along the track

E. Ethelbert Miller

Winnie

this time the fire did not reach my heart
when the cameras and reporters came
i had already picked through the rubble
i found a wedding gift
pictures of our children
lying in the ashes
the earth they call south africa
the land i love but cannot own

nelson
tonight

i no longer wait for your release
i no longer wait for the rumor or the promise
i have accepted the loneliness of courage
i have accepted the loneliness of struggle
even when my own people come to burn my home
i will open my arms in welcome
for my love extends to them also
i will forgive them just as africa must forgive me
if ever i stop and say i cannot go on
my dear
nelson
what does it matter if we lose this life
i dream of tomorrows without funerals
even as your hair turns gray
when you smile i am reminded of that morning
after our marriage
when you promised me a free south africa
and I knew i would love you until death

The Weather

on elevators
on the bus
in front of the store and house
old folks talk about the weather
rain and heat
all the time they talk
about the weather
once long ago
when no man owned the land
the color in the sky was filled with omens
a change in color
could feed or starve a man
when there was no rain
the ground cracked open
old folks took to sitting near the trees
there they would talk
about the weather
and when it rained
they would talk
about the land
the richness and the wealth
how the harvest
would be good
now on concrete streets
in rented homes
old folks curse the rain
they talk about the weather
they have no memory
of the land

E. Ethelbert Miller

Untitled

beirut
like when the new york
yankees terrorized the
american league
the tanks of israel
push back the palestinians

outside lebanon
no one asks for
autographs

The Door

the day after the national election
the sky cleared and the sun found its guitar.
i ran to the plaza and soon discovered myself
dancing in the middle of a jublilant crowd.
a nation of song, a nation of thousands pushing
like the sea to the cathedral. i felt the sweet
sweat of arms, legs and chests. i found my place
among the living, the dead, the ghosts, the children
waiting to be born. something more powerful than
victory was in the air. i could breathe again.
my prison door was open. my country was outside.
she had been waiting for me.

E. Ethelbert Miller

August Rain

it is christmas
somewhere. somewhere i can finally take
my boots off, stare at my filthy feet and wonder
if i will die under a sky i want so desperately to love.
the clouds of my country are so evasive, so female.
i sit for hours watching them circle the mountains.
when news came about the new cease fire i closed my eyes
and slept for the first time in weeks. in my dreams i
made love to a woman, her breath and tongue covering my
body like soft august rain. i awoke and found strands
of her hair drifting in the sky like something from
a cloud, untouchable. i wept face down in the grass
disguising myself as a corpse. i want to be home, to be
away from the earth, to be anywhere but here. i pull
an old scab off a new wound, unwrapping myself like a
gift.

The Sea

neruda once told me
that i should visit the sea
that to know a wave is to love
is to come and flow from one to another
the sand is like our hearts
so many parts to care for
so endless and yet it touches the sea
as one

E. Ethelbert Miller

Migrant Worker

a migrant worker   me
i pass push through the crowd
someone hands me a handout a flyer
telling me to either beware
or become involved
i continue to pass push through the crowd
drop the paper to the ground
a foot covers it
then it's gone
me i'm still here

some speaker is speaking through his mike
i can't understand
can't hear
funny i don't even care
cause
the thrill is gone
and i'm just passing through
picking up slogans
humming the songs of last year's harvest

i'm a migrant worker
looking for a home a job
some cause to believe in
but the thrill is gone

words rain on me
steady and consistent
there has always been clouds
the world is overcast
gone gray   lifeless

there is nothing in this land
that will grow without the nourishment
of blood
that has grown without the nourishment
of blood

i pass push through the crowd
a migrant worker
speaking a language
that has no words
me   i want to yell
join hands   demonstrate
free my brothers around the world
free the world around my brothers
but the thrill is gone

a migrant worker
i pass push through the crowd
reach another city
come to this same place
like a hitchhiker
thumbs out on a highway

i don't drive
i don't demonstrate
i don't even believe what folks
be telling me
a migrant worker   i don't even belong here
the guy with the flyers
who is he?   does he know my name?
i don't take nothing from nobody
i don't drive
i don't demonstrate

E. Ethelbert Miller

i barely believe   believe me

i just want to work   earn my pay   make my way
i believe in america more than i believe in myself
me i'm a migrant worker
i've done seen everything
done everything
only reason i'm here is because
the thrill is gone

i don't pick cotton
i don't pick fruit
i pick winners and losers
and stay away from both

CHINATOWN

Another Love Affair/Another Poem

it was afterwards
when we were in the shower
that she said

"you're gonna write a poem about this?"

"about what?" i asked

Personal #1975

when
between
her
legs

i think
of scissors

cutting

E. Ethelbert Miller

Solo

(for rhonda)

she has nothing to wear
only her dancing fits her body
the movement is all fabric
tight against the flesh
she moves from chair to bed
eyes like notes
soft
harmonic
playful

this is our solo
lips against lips
tongue against tongue

my fingers fingering her body

i play all melody
slow
fast
jazz and blues

i dress her with music
press her breasts like keys

Poem Looking For A Reader

if poems
could undress
you

i would not
hesitate
to ask
or find
words to place
in my hands

sitting
in a room
trying to
write
is like
daydreaming
about your
body

a
comma
separates
your
legs

the
problem
with paper
is that
it has
no

E. Ethelbert Miller

openings

i am
tired
of touching
the surface
of things

there must
be other ways
to love

Song For My Lady, or Excuse Me McCoy

i am tired of women who love musicians
who desire to be loved by musicians
who think that musicians are the best lovers
and the best players
i am tired
and do not care to listen to this anymore
do not sing to me or hum to me
or proclaim to me a new music
there is NO music
coltrane is dead
parker is dead
navarro is dead
young is dead
cannonball has just died and
so have herbie sanders and benson
and i don't even listen to radio
i am so tired
of women sitting in clubs
sipping drinks of coke and rum
pretending to be billie bessie betty or whomever
laying around between acts
being very hip
i am very tired
of the woman who tells me that the man
she loves is in europe
back from europe
or heading for europe
i am tired of music lovers

E. Ethelbert Miller

coming down from new york
telling me about the apple
if you are william tell please do not take aim at my head
i am tired and need no second headaches
i do not need another woman to tell me
that what's hers belongs to the drummer
and what's mine is fine
but it just don't swing
i am tired of telling women
that i am better than bebop
that what i got is the new thing
that i can play an instrument as good as anyone
i am tired of telling them this
so from now on
whenever i hear a woman
talking about some musician
about how way-out his sound is
about how his music gets all up inside and-moves her around
from now on when i hear a woman talking about a muscian
i'm gonna turn my back like miles
pull my hat down like monk
disappear like rollins
and maybe come back next year
if i feel like it and if she's ready

First Light

The Feeling Of Jazz

what would ellington
say if he saw us walking
across his bridge? your
hands pushed deep into
your pockets. my hat a
funny one like the kind
musicians wear. i can
see duke being majestic,
wondering if we're lovers.
how else to explain this
closeness between our coats.

E. Ethelbert Miller

She Is Flat On Her Back
(for k. f.)

she is flat on her back
when she decides/she decides
it's time to make that move
she rises from the bed
she says

       i'll be right back
        i'm not protected

and it is at that time/now
i wonder about the danger that i am
the terrible thing i must be
that she needs to be protected
and it is not the fear of children
the fear of having children
it is me
that she fears/i think

as i lie in the dark
staring at the ceiling
listening to her move around
in the bathroom
the opening of closets
the sound of water
the turning on/and off of lights

and now
she is back
next to me
her hand back in place
where she left me

First Light

and i am vulnerable
to love
i am not protected
i am vulnerable to love
        to love

E. Ethelbert Miller

Dressed Up

one day
i'm gonna
be dressed
up in a coffin

have a nice
tie and suit
on

my old
girl friend
won't have
to complain
about me
wearing jeans
every place
i go

one day
when i'm
dressed up
in my coffin

i'm gonna
ask her out

take her
somewhere
she hasn't
been

Poem for RV

when you leave
i realize how much
my life needs air
and how much loving
you would be a reason
for living   why are
you so beautiful?
why do i desire you as
much as air?

E. Ethelbert Miller

We Waited

we
waited
so long
to touch

that fingers
dripped
tears

into
palms

Birds

near lake washington
the afternoon turns warm
with the sun of early spring.

your face, your arms, your legs
turning in your bed
discover mine.

along the lake
birds stare at the windows of our
house. i learn to swim in the
wetness of you.

E. Ethelbert Miller

Where Are My Woman's Wings?

where are my woman's wings?
her songs?
we stand birdlike on limbs searching
the sky for each other.
where is our flock now that we are captured
forced to stare at history from behind bars?
where are my woman's wings?
stolen? the blues dripping from her hair and feathers
i am inside my horn
my slender beak
playing myself into light and bright moments.
do you hear my love song
my song of the sun?
rise my woman rise
fly back to me.
where are your wings?

Moses

her body was on fire beneath his.

her hands on his back scratched words
into his flesh. his shoulders were like
tablets. broad and strong.

they loved
until morning
until daylight forced him from her bed.
out the room and door.

hair uncombed.
it stood like horns upon his head.

an old woman passing
was shocked by his presence

frightened by the fire in his eyes.

E. Ethelbert Miller

Hunters

men
who
chase
after
women

are
like
hunters

who
k i l l
their
prey

upon
capture.

Rebecca

will i hate mirrors?
will i hate reflections?
will i hate to dress?
will i hate to undress?

jim my husband
tells me it won't matter
if i have one or two
two or one it doesn't matter
he says

but it does
i know it does

this is my body
this is not south africa or nicaragua
this is my body
losing a war against cancer
and there are no demonstrators outside
the hospital to scream stop

there is only jim
sitting in the lobby
wondering what to say
the next time we love
and his hands move towards
my one surviving breast

how do we convince ourselves
it doesn't matter?
how do i embrace my own nakedness
now that it is no longer complete?

E. Ethelbert Miller

Linda

i live in a basement apartment
where sunlight squeezes between
earth and blades of grass
everyday my neighbor lets her dog
enjoy the yard in front of my window
i spend the days counting flies

there are times when i debate
with myself about animal rights
i think about life while preparing dinner
i think about my neighbor's dog as i cut
a small chicken into parts

murder is such an easy thing to do
i have never spoken to the people
who live upstairs

i could kill the dog without a witness
i could be the neighbor police question
i could be the fly on the wall

Linda

it got nothing to do with how much
i hate to wash clothes
no i don't mind even if there's no laundry
in my building and the closest one is five blocks away
and a pushcart means you got kids and an army bag
means you're either lazy or dirty but ain't got no other means
or man to help you there...which brings me to a few days ago
when i decided to wash a dress
a slip and some other things
around seven in the evening near wednesday
the middle of the week
so i got all the washers and dryers i need
in fact i got the whole place to myself
but that doesn't last too long
because it's like love or what you think love is
it comes and goes and passes through an open door

this guy
some man
this creature
with his zipper open
this fool with no shirt
no socks
just a scar on his face
stumbles into the laundry without the first thing to wash
except himself
this fool
passes all the machines and stops in front of me and says:

                baby i'm homeless

E. Ethelbert Miller

> take me home
> let me be your man

and i catch the odor of his breath
before i stare at the ceiling and the walls
why me god i ask i just have a dress and slip to wash
i should be five blocks away with my cat curled in my lap
and a cold beer in my hand but here i am among the
colored clothes and whites...so the thing passes by and
crawls into an empty dryer and shuts the door where i
see him peeking through the glass and picking at his nose

but before my prayers are answered
here comes mr. heartache
mr. pain

a young kid slipping and sliding across the floor
you know the type
be a hoodlum
if he wasn't by himself

be a freak
if i wasn't the lady of his dreams
the answer to his:

> hey momma
> are all your sheets
> dirty or are the clean ones
> home waiting just for me?

i listen to the kid's rap
his song without a dance
his words curving against my hips like sound coming from
a jukebox filled with jive

the cool one does a spin so i can check the back of his legs

the sight i'm sure he would leave me with if i was
ten years younger or maybe make it twelve

> hey baby
> look at this
> check this dude in his crib

the slick one spots the crazy guy inside the dryer
he pulls a quarter from his pocket and slips the coin into
the slot

E. Ethelbert Miller

Billie Holiday

sometimes the deaf
hear better than the blind

some men
when they first
heard her sing

were only attracted
to the flower in her hair

Survival Poem

(for june)

when the earth opened
i whispered your name
i prayed for your safety
the distance between us
a slight tremor
our love holding up
against the odds

E. Ethelbert Miller

Pretzels

these women love hard
legs snake around you like pretzels
takin salt off you back
you be sittin on a bus
lookin at nothin
and they think you tryin
to peep their thing
but it be nothin
to look at there
underneath de dress
nothin new under de sun there
only a moist darkness
that will suck you in
then spit you out
you a dripdryin lover
tryin to be a man
twisted like a pretzel
you know?

Just A Kiss In The Dark

nothing makes sense
especially the women i've known
i should have kept a diary
or started writing science fiction
but i fell in love
with movies
and people who say the right thing
at the right time but always leave
i wanted someone to say something
wonderful or maybe
just hold me baby just once
i've always kept my promises
even to women who loved women
and never loved me
i never wanted to be lonely
no one ever does
i only wanted the popcorn
not the kisses in the dark

E. Ethelbert Miller

Poem

when you wake up
consider this relationship
to be the misplacement
of your panties
on some cold morning
when you need them

Poem For Marucha

when kisses find their wings
they will return to our lips
to fly again

E. Ethelbert Miller

Silk

i have known women
to steal my heart and vanish
like master fard
in detroit around 1930

silks the only remains
of some lost religion
i've lost faith in

Poem for Seble

in the refrigerator
the oranges are on the bottom shelf
next to the lettuce and tomatoes.
i think of you and wonder why
i am hungry. it is ten o'clock
and my wife and daughter are asleep
in the next room. i imagine you
sipping wine somewhere in europe.
i pour a glass of juice and change
my mind about eating. i stand in the
kitchen wanting to love you, trying
to forget each dangerous feeling. if
sleep could replace memory i could
think of you tonight and again
as often as one remembers. inside
the refrigerator the grapes are cold
and silent, never have i wanted
so much to be held.

E. Ethelbert Miller

Are You The Woman Of My Dreams?

don't be telling nobody you can't find no man
don't be talking about niggers and faggots
and how somebody always trying to get some from you
you don't know what's really happening
you need some/some of everything
but are you ready?
do you really want to love?
and where is the love you are ready to give?
i want some
but first you better find it
because i don't see it
and something is missing from your eyes
like a strange perfume
you got my nose wide open but something don't smell too
good
you say you want to be loved
you want a man to care/to take care
to be there/not to disappear when you come
i say are you ready?
and will the first lady please stand
and sing something like "lover man" or "now or never"
now or never i'll be your man
don't be looking for me tomorrow
because i will not be here
i will not wait/i will not even hesitate
i will leave you at the station
i will leave you with the bags
unless you give me love
but are you ready?

First Light

do you really want to love?
and where is the love you are ready to give?
don't be saying black men ain't shit and niggers are niggers
because i say
who are you?
are you the woman of my dreams/the queen supreme?
my first /my last/my everything?
my lucky charm/my mistletoe/my ship come in?
my cup runneth over/my lord's response?
i say
who are you?
are you the first commandment or the last straw?
i say
don't be telling nobody you can't find no man
you don't know what's really happening
you should travel
or better yet move next door
maybe you should even read more
i say i could love you
if you could love
now or never
i'll be your man

E. Ethelbert Miller

Shorty's Poem As Told To Dinky

some things make you grow a beard
some things don't
so it was dinky told me or how i remember it
the first summer i went south
colored was all i knew
and colored was what the signs said

i was five and starting to read
find a word first and then a sound
a whole world open to me
like a cute girl crossing her legs

a lot of things i still don't understand
like where aunt martha takes her cat when it's sick
is there a colored animal hospital for coloreds' animals
and a white one for white folk's animals
or is it just some places for cats and another for dogs
dinky says coloreds' animals go
to the regular hospital for coloreds
it don't make no difference if you have four legs or two

tonight i want to believe in jesus
but i don't know how
i found this letter my older sister bess
cut out a magazine

dear essence,
>   i am black and single and have been in prison
>   for fifteen years. i killed my husband and
>   three-month-old baby while
>   i was unemployed. when i am released next month i
>   would like to meet a man. what can i do?

ms. violet

dear ms. violet,

> there are many men waiting to love you. if you can wait
> fifeen years you can wait fifteen more. many of us have
> yet to go to prison.

so i hear my father
tell mr. buster that nellie got some nice legs
so i ring the bell next door and ask for candy one afternoon
just to catch a peek and what i see
don't make me want to whisper

dinky tells me that some women are like the river we fish in
some men catch things and others never learn how to swim
i want to be a sailor when i grow up dinky say
i see him looking at the sun

the river no where in sight
that's why i want to grow a beard
and be a man like mr. buster or my daddy

dear essence,

> i am five years old and have never had sex.
> am i gonna die?

>> shorty

dear shorty,

> i suggest you subscribe to our magazine. if you are
> old enough to read you know that death is something
> many people grow into.
> don't worry we are a monthly publication and
> will give you your money back if you die.

E. Ethelbert Miller

Summer

on hot days
young women
dangle their legs
off stoops
cross ankles
& rock themselves
in tune to music
coming from open
windows

passing men
laugh & joke
if they could
they would
lift those legs
like a warm
summer breeze
and dance

Chinatown

in the morning
she would hold his
hands against the light
translucent hands like the torn
shade at her window
in the morning
she would hold his hands
against the light
like fans from the orient
she would hold them close
to her face

E. Ethelbert Miller

You Must Know What This Is About

while i write
in the middle
of the night

you slip across
the border
into my poem

there are
no passports
to the heart
no documents
to deny entry

inside my poem
you rearrange
my life

you hold my
imagination
in your hands

Killing Me Softly

all i listen to is roberta flack
her voice singing the way i want to walk
i hold my hands against my eyes
hoping i will see the love or even the face
of my mother

people hold my hand
but only to give me direction
i want to do more than cross a street
or find my way through a crowd

i want to be in love
i want someone to touch me the way i touch
the way i see things in the darkness that
is always there

what color is love?
what does it look like?

i listen to roberta flack and i imagine
a handsome man to be the outline
of something beautiful like the taking
of a first step or traveling alone without a cane
the world a symphony of sound
each note as distinct as a small dot on a page

i place my hands on a book and feel
the braille letters like the uneven surface
of a lover's arms and legs

i bring the book slowly to my lips
i kiss the page and whisper

"when will a man open his eyes to me?"

E. Ethelbert Miller